good grief

Good Grief ©2019 by **Mikey Swanberg**. Published in the United States by Vegetarian Alcoholic Press. Not one part of this work may be reproduced without expressed written consent from the author. For more information, please contact vegalpress@gmail.com

Cover art and title page by Emily Louise Howard

For Rebecca, Jane, and Nikky –

Table of Contents

Good Grief..............………………….9

Under the fluorescent sun
it is always Southern California
inside the Kroger.

- Jane Gentry Vance 1995

    A bath when you're born
a bath when you die,
    how stupid.

- Kobayashi Issa 1828
-     Translated by Robert Hass

*

(Jane)   the greeks said
  a lot of things

like *if you're looking*
  for a jackdaw

one is always
  hanging out

with other jackdaws
  or *doctor*   *goddamnit*   *cure yourself*

they believed in a lament
  you should never name the dead

for fear of waking them
  for fear a sweet thing tasted

too often is no longer
  very sweet

but it's not true
  of course   of you

I don't think
  that's true of anything

*

    I wish you were here
        to hear how the ice cleaved

    into sheets like candied glass
        then broke

    though no one got hurt
        & no one got dead

    & we all went home
        through our own bootpaths

    with buckets & coolers
        full of wide-eyed fish

    who seeing the sun
        undazzled by water

    thought a bath in oil
        might do the trick

*

but you are not here
   & spring came on

with bad fights   though
   once really happy

with a sunburn
   & the cards on the table

& the wind dying down
   & even the black ice birdsong

off the heating lake
   creaked open like itself for once

I was happy
   in a way I so rarely am

so I said
   I am happy

just to let it
   all melt off

*

(Jane)   the years stack
   like clear plates

I can still see everything
   that happened

warped
   & slightly pink

we become ourselves slowly
   though it doesn't feel like that

we order french fries
   we shit talk   we keep packing

our bags for a trip
   we never take

*

we say

*often I was lonely
and often I was
lonesome and there is
a difference because one*

*needs country music
and the other
needs the sound*

*of the
fridge clicking*

off

*

(Jane)　the postcard you sent
　a decade ago

a Hopper　stays tucked
　in my mirror　a woman sitting nude

in her room　the day's light slanting in
　& her gazing at me in mine

getting dressed for work
　trying something on & frowning

trying something else

*

you don't want to die
  a mother says into a phone

my mother
  my phone

I didn't say that   I said
  I feel like I want to die

sometimes I feel
  like having a pizza

& it doesn't
  mean anything

*

we take nothing with us
  I know because

the grave is no roomier
  than a twin

but when my girlfriend & I split
  there was still the matter of the mattress

our mattress
  & the good beer cups

our good beer cups
  & the hours

like cheap cookies
  breaking to crumbs

all through the apartment
  as we tried again

to break apart ourselves
  you can take anything

you want if you just wipe down
  the shelves

*

(Jane)   love dies like a tooth
   years of bad care

and then all at once
   a shout

and the whole month is wrecked
   and graying fast

it never helps
   that there are others

*

*it's okay   my friend later said   to turn
   over a new leaf*

*yeah
   but look what happens when I do*

*it's just the shittier
   side of the same leaf*

*

I tried to type
   to my friend

I am sorry
   but I am incompetent

but the phone
   had other plans

& shone blue to me

I am sorry
   but I am incomplete

*

oh (Jane)   I went out looking for extra mothers
  & found them everywhere I turned

but what did I learn about myself
  beyond my bottomless need

to be directed
  & soothed

like some night creature knocking
  his nail on the glass

in the book I read over and over
  as a boy   a bird walks

up to a piece of construction equipment & asks
  wait   are you my mother?

*

so when I was my saddest
   I asked   *how is it I become more*

& more handsome
  the sadder I get

& bless those I love
  for never saying

oh come on honey
  you didn't

*

those last months
   when you were going

like a house in sand
   I called often to hear

your voicemail-box was full
   I called to be relieved

there was nothing to say

*

(Jane)   I am not sorry
   I'm incomplete

if I'm being completely
   honest   it is probably

the only bright thing
   about me

*

it's okay that everything is shit
   I say to the side yard & recycling bins

there is still Hopper
   the cities still swell

with the lonely who still pause
   to watch the light

from a window cross
   the still-nude back of the wall

if we are frozen here
   by some greater hand

it hasn't seemed to bother us at all

*

some ideas of what the birds could be doing
on the power lines

having a meeting
waiting for a meeting to start
finishing up their early meeting

*

(Jane)   I can say it
   this is a lament after all

after all this time   I still feel rudderless
   after all this time   I still google lament

to make sure I am saying
   what I think I am

*

what the heart knows now
   the body knows eventually

& so we pace
   the same bright blocks

the seasons try
   and try again

to make untrue
   what was

always always
   true

*

(Jane)   in the half frozen river
   a seagull stood on a submarine

sandwich floating past
   convinced it was a log

& I   ever impressed
   with late-stage environmentalism

would not dare
   to call him wrong

*

Oh (Jane) it's no surprise
   but no man ever taught me

to like the world
   or to like myself in it

that job was left to the women
   of Kentucky who saw my goat's heart

& didn't mind I was still a kid

*

(Jane)   sometimes I get down
   & I drag my fat body

all over the wood floor
   & I think   this is all

about a lack
   of institutional memory

but then I think
   of all the books I read

& didn't like & I know
   the problem is me

*

I wish I had cried
   when the dental hygienist said

pain is a good teacher
   after the nerve in my tooth

had panicked & died
   but I was cried out from that
whole week

& couldn't eat anything
   but water & beer

& didn't care
   if she was being profound

or just selling me something
   I was tired

I asked for an itemized list
   of what every step would cost

*

oh (Jane)   once as a boy
   I found an old trunk in the garbage

& was sure there must be something
   good inside

& I need to tell you this so that you know
   that I was always an idiot

*

I came back
  & you were frail

& sick
  & you looked rough

& I said   *you look good*
  I am glad

you look so good

*

a girlfriend & I pretend
  in the hotel

to have undergone a tragedy
  to make the other laugh

we misheard a country song as
  I was a hot mess

when my son had passed
  we had been fighting all day

but for a moment
  that fish scale thin territory

between what is funny & what is hard
  fell away enough to let down our guard

*

(Jane)

the world was beautiful
  & mysterious & the

people were mostly cuties
  & fun & I

was bad often
  to those that

loved me best
  & just

as often
   forgiven

*

the river froze &
   then the lake froze

& then the sidewalk
   chunked up with gray

ice thick as
   coiled snakes &

cold & still
   we walked

smiling toward
   home

*

oh   come back
  I know you can't

but I want some task
  from the other side

bigger than the dishes
  or just to be kind

I am tired all the time

the sun comes in my room
  like a bossy asshole

& pushes the papers around
  & licks at my eyeball

until I say   *okay okay okay*
  I'm up

*

when I asked *how many chickadees*
  it would take to carry

a hamburger bun from the dusty street
  to the shortleaf pine

I wasn't proposing
  some thought exercise

I saw it myself
  the answer is five

*

this land is your
   land   we say first

& then we remind
   you that   *this land*

is my land
   & we lay

out from where
   to where

and it's
   the whole damn pie

*

(Jane)   was the lesson of poetry to never be happy
   that has been the lesson everywhere else

save the movieplex & the city gardens
   where I go often

just to smell good smells
   & be alone & phoneless

so that I can remember
   that there is nothing hornier

than to watch the bee go down on the flower
   & that any of us can hang out there

with him as long as we need
   just honeying it in

*

for so long I cooked
   nothing that lived

ate nothing
   with kids

but it wasn't the honest smell
   of frying chicken that did me in

not even the ice cream scoop
   as big as a peach

I remembered that
   if I wanted to be in this world

if I was really going
   to be of it

I was going to have to mean
   the end of something

*

oh (Jane)　　& isn't that all so awful
　　the white plums & the bean birds

& the way that everything lays us low

I want a weed gummi
　　& to be handled

instead I settle for bad news
　　from my phone all day long

you wrote

> *all we beasts*
> *familiar to each other*
> *as plain as being*
> *and strange*
>
> *all of us*
> *what we were*
> *what we are*

& just today I slapped the hood of a car
　　that by not seeing me

wished me dead

> all of us
> what we were
> what we are

what a way that'd have been
 for this to end

*

(Jane)   I know I am trying
   to replace you with your own words

to put a voice to what only comes on
   as a bored & creaky pain

did I ever even learn a thing from you

because the river   *does*   looks like a ribbon
   from the silver bullet of the plane

the country below   our country
   all virgin scraggly wood & rock

is just a teenager
   turning into a wolf

then turning back again

*

I promised that I wouldn't write
   angry & I promised that I wouldn't

write with the censor
   in the room &

I promised that I wouldn't write
   that the heart

is a bright
   blue bird

still flapping   falling
   somewhere

*

so instead like Moses
   I learned the laws

I indemnified the self
   against negligence

against omissions
   against yet to be named disasters

I said no matter what happens
   we get our money back

*

(Jane)   come back
  to lead our pack

those wolves in Kentucky
  are just dogs

half stray   half mad
  from howling

at the   bright   round   clock
  on top of the bank

*

(Jane)   you knew well enough
   how weak with words

our grief can leave us
   so you wrote it plain

we do not pass
   we die

but time passes
   & so I do look up Hopper

who said   *maybe I am not very human*
   what I wanted to do

was paint sunlight
   on the side of a house

*

I know how
  this will sound

like a bird
  proud of a bird bush

but before we bow our heads to eat
  I add   blue/grass/grief

to my shortlist
  of near perfect things

*

so maybe I too am not
  very human

a woman was throwing
  her boyfriend's clothes

out the window
  & into the street

& I mistaking them for autumn leaves
  asked   *is it fall already*

*

(Jane)   is what I want
   to admit that love

is a distraction   & that we
   in love   are glad for a moment

just not to be lost
   I know there are no good outcomes

I hear you as you say
   oh Mikey

aren't you just talking at a woman
   who can't even start to talk back

*

but (Love)   I've tired
  && you would not know me

so full of right angles
   to find love

is to feel your own hand
   unfastening the belt   & to stay

in love is to become
   a magician's knot

& to unwind & unwind
   with each biting thought

*

(Jane)   would you have stood
   for this

all those semesters we wrote
   the rules

as you chalked them into being
   but it seems   after all this time

that the biggest one
   of them got lost

how many times
   did I write it for myself

avoid sentimentality at all costs

*

    but I am sentimental
       you are sentimental

    they are sentimental
       we are sentimental

*

oh (Jane)   I got it wrong before
   so much   so what

being alive
   is as good as licking

a knuckle of garlic as thick
   as the queen

we only need to feel good
     about it   we don't

need to know
   what it means

*

so it's with awe I watch
  the couple in the coffee shop

break up
  then un break up

oh heart
  take two with breakfast

take comfort
  take this little cardboard sleeve

*

it is late now
   and time to say

that I read Hopper & his wife Jo
   beat the living shit

out of each other
   and maybe he ruined her career

or maybe   as some friends have said
   she was happy just to model for him

and catalogue his paintings
   to both be & record their provenance

I don't really buy that
   but the best I can do

is to offer up
   this

you don't know shit about a marriage
   if you're not in it

*

(Jane)   was I supposed to kill my starlings
   was I supposed to tell it plain

who knows

what you taught was
   how best to enjoy an artichoke

how not to ruin that
   with poems

*

that which we begin
  in grief cannot be

finished in grief   you
  cannot mourn the house

you are building
  and expect it

to stand
  until you thank

every chatty
  plank

*

(Jane)   this was all a gift
    & I was one of your luckier kids

so I will not end
    on a flash or trick

I will not slip out the door
    to sip some beer

I was lucky to learn what
    you showed up to show us

that as bad as it gets
    we are lucky

to get to be together
    right here

*

the greeks were wrong
  about grief

but I get where they stood
  on pain

because they don't say
  to make your life hell

they say   *to make your life
  a roller-skate*

Thanks!

To all my friends and poetry friends in Kentucky, Chicago, Wisconsin, and New York – and all my writing teachers -- this book couldn't exist without you! Thanks Kate Hadfield, Vincent Elliott, Clay Spencer, Corrinne Keel, Chuck Clenny, Emily Howard, Jess Cullen, Bianca Bargo, Kasia & Andre Pater, Jared Baize, Amy Lipman, Ashley Keyser, Kyle Chipman, Zac Fulton, Sean Bishop, Jesse Lee Kercheval, Ron Wallace, Amy Quan Barry, Amuad Jamal Johnson, Meg Wade, Caitlin Quinn, and Derick Mattern. Thanks to Greg Lamer and Robin LaMer Rahija who saved this book from the brink many many times. Thanks to Stef & Matt Daigler, Katie Yelick, Steve Minogue, Chris & Alma, John McDonough & Annie Strother and all the participants of poetry month. Thanks Sam Pekarske, Woodland Pattern, Sandy Duffy, and Lindsay Daigle. Thanks Franklin K.R. Cline for making pretty much every good poetry thing in the last 3 years happen! Thanks to all my family! Thanks Freddy La Force for wanting to make the book you are holding now, and for seeing a bunch of small poems as something bigger! And Thanks Liv Stratman, who keeps showing me new ways to be an artist year after year.

Mikey Swanberg holds an MFA from the University of Wisconsin - Madison, and is the author of the chapbook *Zen & The Art of Bicycle Delivery* (Rabbit Catastrophe Press). He lives and works in Chicago.

www.ingramcontent.com/pod-product-compliance
Lightning Source LLC
Chambersburg PA
CBHW060506080526
44584CB00015B/1570